# Stars & Ribbons

## CRIB QUILTS

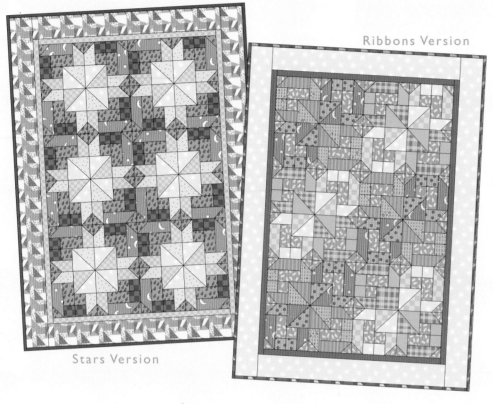

Stars Version

Ribbons Version

**Stars & Ribbons Crib Quilts**
*Finished Size: 43" x 59"*
*Photo of Stars Version on page 1, Ribbons Version on page 5*

*Stars or ribbons—you choose! This versatile quilt pattern will give you two
distinctly different effects depending on your fabric selection! Pastel ribbons
or bright stars take center stage in this easily pieced crib-size quilt.
We've provided cutting charts and directions for both versions.
Make them both ... nobody will guess that they're the same pattern!*

## Making the Blocks

You will be making twenty-four blocks: twelve of Block 1 and twelve of Block 2. Refer to Quilt Layout above for color placement. Whenever possible use the Assembly Line Method described on page 22. Press in direction of arrows.

## Instructions for Block 1

**1.** Refer to Quick Corner Triangle directions on page 22. Sew 2½" Fabric A square to 2½" x 6½" Fabric B piece. Press.

A = 2½ x 2½
B = 2½ x 6½
Make 12

**2.** Sew 2½" Fabric C square to 2½" x 4½" Fabric A piece. Press.

2½   4½

 2½

← Make 12

**3.** Referring to diagram, sew units from step 1 to units from step 2. Press.

**4.** Make Quick Corner Triangle unit by sewing 2½" Fabric A square to 2½" x 4½" Fabric D piece. Press.

A = 2½ x 2½
D = 2½ x 4½
Make 12

**5.** Sew units from step 3 to units from step 4. Press.

←

**6.** Sew 2½" Fabric C square to 2½" Fabric A square. Press.

2½   2½

   2½

→ Make 12

**7.** Make Quick Corner Triangle unit by sewing 2½" Fabric A square to 2½" x 4½" Fabric D piece. Press.

→

A = 2½ x 2½
D = 2½ x 4½
Make 12

*To make a twin-size quilt, sew five rows with three units each & adjust your borders as desired.*

## STARS VERSION

# Fabric Requirements and Cutting Instructions

Before you begin, read Cutting the Strips and Pieces on page 22.

| | | First Cut | | Second Cut | |
| --- | --- | --- | --- | --- | --- |
| | | Number of Strips or Pieces | Dimensions | Number of Pieces | Dimensions |
| Fabric A Background 3/4 yard | | 9 | 2½" x 42" | 24 | 2½" x 4½" |
| | | | | 96 | 2½" squares |
| Fabric B Block Corners Light 1/3 yard | | 4 | 2½" x 42" | 24 | 2½" x 6½" |
| Fabric C Block Corners Dark 1/3 yard | | 3 | 2½" x 42" | 48 | 2½" squares |
| Fabric D Star Center and Points 1/2 yard | | 1 | 5½" x 42" | 6 | 5½" squares |
| | | 3 | 2½" x 42" | 24 | 2½" x 4½" |
| Fabric E Star Center and Points 1/2 yard | | 1 | 5½" x 42" | 6 | 5½" squares |
| | | 3 | 2½" x 42" | 24 | 2½" x 4½" |
| Fabric F Star Center 3/8 yard | | 2 | 5½" x 42" | 12 | 5½" squares |
| **Borders** | | | | | |
| | Accent Border 1/3 yard | 5 | 1½" x 42" | | |
| | Outside Border 3/4 yard | 5 | 4½" x 42" | | |
| | Binding 1/2 yard | 6 | 2¾" x 42" | | |
| Backing - 3 yards Batting - 51" x 67" | | | | | |

**8.** Sew units from step 6 to units from step 7. Press.

**9.** Use a ruler to draw diagonal line on wrong side of 5½" Fabric E square. Place Fabric E square and 5½" Fabric F square right sides together. Sew seams ¼" away from diagonal line on both sides to make half square triangles. Make six.

Cut on diagonal line and press toward Fabric F. Trim to 4½". This will make two half-square triangles.

E = 5½ x 5½
F = 5½ x 5½
Trim to 4½
Make 12

**10.** Sew units from step 8 to units from step 9 as shown. Press.

**11.** Sew units from step 5 to units from step 10. Press. Blocks measure 8½" square. Make twelve.

**12.** Lay out cut fabrics following diagram for color placement of Block 2. Repeat steps 1-11 to make twelve of Block 2 substituting Fabric E for Fabric D in steps 4 and 7 and substituting Fabric D for Fabric E in step 9.

## Assembly

**1.** Following diagram, sew Block 1 to Block 2. Press. Make twelve sets.

Block 1    Block 2

Make 12

**2.** Sew units from step 1 together in pairs. Press. Make six blocks.

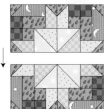

Make 6

**3.** Referring to layout on page 2 and color photo on page 1, sew units from step 2 together in pairs to make three rows. Sew rows together.

## Borders

**1.** Measure quilt through center from side to side. Cut two 1¹/₂" x 42" accent border strips to that measurement. Sew to top and bottom. Press seams toward border strips.

**2.** Cut one 1¹/₂" x 42" accent border strip in half. Sew to one end of each remaining accent border strip.

**3.** Measure quilt through center from top to bottom including borders just added. Cut two 1¹/₂" accent border strips to that measurement. Sew to sides. Press.

**4.** Repeat steps 1-3 to attach outside border strip. Press.

## Layering and Finishing

**1.** Cut backing fabric crosswise into two equal pieces. Sew pieces together to make one 54" x 84" (approximate) backing piece. Arrange and baste backing, batting, and top together referring to Layering the Quilt directions on page 24.

**2.** Machine or hand quilt as desired.

**3.** Sew 2³/₄" x 42" binding strips end to end to make one continuous strip. Refer to Binding the Quilt directions on page 24 and use the pieced binding strips to finish.

## RIBBONS VERSION

## Fabric Requirements and Cutting Instructions

Before you begin, read Cutting the Strips and Pieces on page 22.

| | | First Cut | | Second Cut | |
|---|---|---|---|---|---|
| | | Number of Strips or Pieces | Dimensions | Number of Pieces | Dimensions |
| | Fabric A Background *3/4 yard* | 9 | 2¹/₂" x 42" | 24 96 | 2¹/₂" x 4¹/₂" 2¹/₂" squares |
| | Fabric B 4 dark fabrics *3/8 yard each of four different colors* *Repeat cutting for each fabric* | 1 2 | 5¹/₂" x 42" 2¹/₂" x 42" | 3 6 6 | 5¹/₂" squares 2¹/₂" x 6¹/₂" 2¹/₂" x 4¹/₂" |
| | Fabric C 4 light fabrics *3/8 yard each of four different colors* *Repeat cutting for each fabric* | 1 2 | 5¹/₂" x 42" 2¹/₂" x 42" | 3 6 12 | 5¹/₂" squares 2¹/₂" x 4¹/₂" 2¹/₂" squares |
| **Borders** | | | | | |
| | Accent Border *1/3 yard* | 5 | 1¹/₂" x 42" | | |
| | Outside Border *3/4 yard* | 5 | 4¹/₂" x 42" | | |
| | Binding *1/2 yard* | 6 | 2³/₄" x 42" | | |

Backing - 3 yards
Batting - 51" x 67"

## Making the Blocks

You will be making twenty-four blocks in various colors. (Six blocks each in purple, coral, green, and yellow.) Refer to Quilt Layout on page 2 for color placement.

Whenever possible use the Assembly Line Method described on page 22. Press in direction of arrows.

**1.** Lay out cut fabrics following diagram for color placement.

Make 6 each color

2. Referring to Making the Blocks instructions for the Stars Version of the Stars & Ribbons Quilt on page 2, sew quilt blocks as shown. Sub-stitute Fabric C for Fabric D in step 4, Fabric B for Fabric D in step 7, and Fabrics B/C for Fabrics E/F in step 9.

3. Following diagram, sew Blocks 1, 2, 3, and 4 together. Press. Make three sets.

Row 1

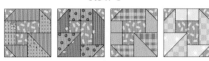

Block 1 → Block 2 → Block 3 → Block 4

Make 3

4. Following diagram, sew Blocks 2, 1, 4, and 3 together. Press. Make three sets.

Row 2

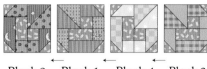

Block 2 ← Block 1 ← Block 4 ← Block 3

Make 3

5. Referring to Quilt Layout on page 2, sew one set from step 3 to one set from step 4. Press. Repeat to make three rows.

6. Arrange and sew rows together following Quilt Layout on page 2. Press.

7. Follow border directions for the Stars Version of the Stars & Ribbons Quilt on page 4 and Layering and Finishing the Quilt instructions on page 4 to finish the quilt.

# Moonbeam
## ACCENT PILLOW

*Finished Size: 18 1/2" x 18 1/2"*

## Fabric Requirements

Background (3/8 yard) - One 11" square
Inside Borders (1/2 yard) - Four 3 1/2" x 22" strips
Outside Border (1/4 yard) - Four 1 1/2" x 22" strips
Lining & Batting (5/8 yard) - One 21 1/2" square
Backing (1/2 yard) - Two 12 3/4" x 18 1/2" pieces

## Making the Pillow

1. Sew inside border strips and outside border strips together lengthwise in pairs.

2. Add borders to 11" background fabric square using Mitered Borders directions on page 24.

3. Refer to Quick-Fuse Appliqué directions on page 23. Trace appliqué designs from pages 8 and 18. Referring to photo for placement, quick-fuse appliqués to pillow top. Machine stitch or use a blanket stitch to finish edges.

4. Layer batting between pillow top and lining. Baste. Hand or machine quilt as desired. Trim batting and lining even with raw edge of pillow top.

5. Narrow hem one long edge of each 12 1/2" x 18 1/2" backing piece.

6. With right side up, lay one backing piece over second piece so hemmed edges overlap. Baste pieces together at top and bottom where they overlap.

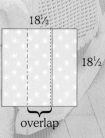

18 1/2

18 1/2

overlap

7. With right sides together, position and pin pillow top to backing. Sew around edges, trim corners, turn right side out, and press. Insert 18" pillow form.

# Stars & Moons

## WINDOW COVERING

Stars & Moons Window Covering

*Star Light, Star Bright, the first star you see tonight will be framed in the window! Soft-sculpted stars and moons hang from ribbons to form a valance. A whimsical border print highlights the curtain. This window covering is fast and easy and baby will love the nursery rhyme feel!*

## Fabric Requirements

Curtains - Width: 2 times
   width of window plus 4"
Length: desired length plus 6"

## Assembly

**1.** Measure width of window. Multiply this figure by 2 and add 4" to obtain the curtain width.

**2.** Measure desired length of finished curtain. Add 6" to this measurement to obtain curtain length.

**3.** Cut fabric to these measurements.

**4.** On side of curtain fabric, turn under ⅝" and press. Turn under an additional ⅝". Press and stitch. Repeat for other side.

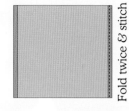

Fold twice & stitch

**5.** Turn under the bottom edge of curtain ½" to wrong side. Press. Turn under an additional ½", press and stitch.

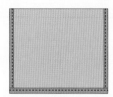

**6.** Turn under ¼" along the top edge. Press and stitch. Turn under an additional 4" along the top edge, placing wrong sides together. Press. Sew across top edge of curtain 1½" away from folded edge, forming top edge of casing.

**7.** Measure width or diameter of curtain rod and add ½". Mark this measurement below first stitching line and stitch to form rod pocket. Press and place on rod.

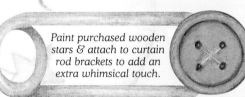

*Paint purchased wooden stars & attach to curtain rod brackets to add an extra whimsical touch.*

## Stars & Moons

For our narrow window, we made two moons and three stars. If your window is wider, you may want to make more of each. A different expression appears on each side of the moon; one is awake and the other is asleep.

## Fabric Requirements

Moons - ¼ yard (cut 2–8" x 20" pieces)
Hats - ⅙ yard (cut 2–5" x 20" pieces)
Stars - ¼ yard (cut 3–7" x 13½" pieces)
Cheek stars - scraps
Ribbon (¼"-wide) - 2–3 yards
    (depending on size of window)
Optional: Buttons for eyes
Embroidery Floss - Blue
Template plastic or paper
Fiberfill
Small Brass Cup Hooks - 5

## Assembly

1. Sew one 8" x 20" moon fabric piece lengthwise to one 5" x 20" hat fabric piece. Repeat to make two.

2. Trace Moon and Star patterns from pages 7 and 8 on paper or template plastic making sure to mark eyes, mouth, ribbon placement, and opening. Cut out templates.

3. Fold fabric right sides together aligning hat seam lines. Place template on wrong side of fabric, aligning template hat line over the seam line, and trace around moon template.

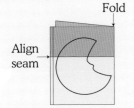

Fold

Align
seam

4. Stitch on traced line leaving open between dots. Trim fabric ¼" away from stitching line. Clip curves and turn right side out.

5. Transfer mouth and eye markings onto moon. We made one side awake and the opposite asleep. Quick-fuse cheek stars to moons referring to directions on page 23. Finish cheek stars with blanket stitching.

**Option:** Embroider now or after moons are stuffed.

6. Stuff moon to desired thickness. Hand stitch opening closed, inserting ribbon for hanging. Repeat steps 3-6 for second moon.

7. Fold each of three 7" x 14" star fabrics with right sides together. Trace around star template onto each fabric. Transfer mouth and eye markings onto star.

**Option:** Embroider star faces now, or after stuffing.

8. Stitch on traced line leaving open between dots. Trim fabric ¼" away from stitching line. Clip curves and turn right side out.

*Make extra Moons & Stars to hang from ceiling over the crib for a mobile.*

9. Stuff to desired thickness. Hand stitch opening closed and stitch on ribbon for hanging. Repeat to make three.

10. Arrange stars and moons as desired and tie with bows to small cup hooks that have been screwed into the window casing.

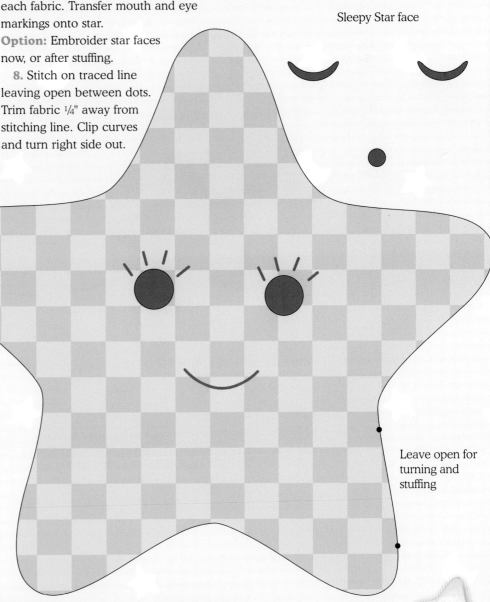

Sleepy Star face

Leave open for turning and stuffing

Leave open for turning and stuffing

Ribbon placement

Hat

Hat seam line

## Tips for Moons & Stars

*Measure your window to determine the length of ribbon for hanging your Moons and Stars. To add interest to your window, place soft sculptures at different levels.*

*Make one soft sculpture to tie to your door handle. Display the "sleepy" side when baby is sleeping to let visitors know not to disturb and the "awake" side when it is okay to visit.*

Awake moon eye placement

Use Moon 100% for Stars & Moons Window Covering.
Reduce Moon to 80% for Fairy Tale Crib Canopy.
Reduce Moon to 80% and reverse for Swinging on a Star Lampshade.
Reduce Moon to 90% for Moonbeam Accent Pillow.

Star for Table Lamp and Moon & Stars Ornament

# Swinging on a Star

## TABLE LAMP

*Stars fall from the shade and swing gently below to catch baby's eyes on this charming table lamp. Stripes and checks in nursery colors highlight the wooden base and decorative braid trims the celestial shade.*

## Materials Needed

Purchased wooden lamp
Lampshade in appropriate size
Multi-colored cording - approx. 2-3 yards
Felted wool or felt - ⅛ yard
Acrylic paints and paintbrushes
Scotch Magic™ Tape
Fabric scraps for moon, hat, and
   cheek-star
Embroidery floss
Heavyweight fusible web - ¼ yard
Spray varnish
Fabric adhesive

## Painting the Lamp Base

Select a wooden lamp base that has an interesting design. Our lamp came from a national discount store and it was already painted a soft vanilla color with a matte finish. If lamp has a glossy finish, it should be sanded before painting. We used a variety of pastel acrylic paints that matched our fabrics to paint portions of the lamp, taking advantage of the existing pattern of the base. Use Scotch Magic™ Tape to mask off areas before you paint. In one wider area, we painted a checkerboard pattern. Measure the area and use a ruler to mark two rows of checks. Paint every other check with blue paint in a checkerboard fashion. When paint is thoroughly dry, spray lamp base with varnish to protect your paint job.

## Embellishing the Lamp Shade

1. Sweet swinging stars and a sleepy moon embellish our lampshade. Reduce the moon pattern on page 8 to 80% and reverse. Trace moon on fabric and cut out. Refer to Quick-Fuse Appliqué directions on page 23. Trace hat and cheek-star templates on paper-side of fusible web and fuse to fabrics selected, following manufacturer's instructions. Cut out hat and cheek-star. Fuse to moon according to the pattern placement. Using embroidery floss, embroider eyes and mouth and add blanket stitches around the cheek-star. Using fabric adhesive, adhere moon to the lampshade.

2. Using heavyweight fusible web, fuse two pieces of felted wool or felt together following manufacturer's directions. Trace star on page 8 onto template plastic. Cut out and use template to draw stars on the fused felt. Cut out stars. We used eight stars around the bottom of the lampshade (approximately 5" apart) and two on the shade. You may need more stars depending on the size of your lampshade. Stitch stars to shade leaving approximately ¼" thread showing so stars can hang freely.

3. Measure top and bottom circumference of shade to determine yardage for trim. Use a permanent fabric adhesive to apply trim to lamp.

# Precious Memories
## PICTURE FRAMES

*Wonderful artwork is found on Debbie Mumm® greeting cards, so select a few of your favorites and frame them to add a special touch to the nursery. Paint frames in nursery colors and accent each one with simple designs inspired by the cards.*

## Materials Needed

Unfinished wooden picture frames
Acrylic paints to match your nursery
Assorted paintbrushes
Ruler and pencil
Matte spray varnish
Sandpaper
Stencils (optional)

## Painting the Frames

1. Use sandpaper on wooden frame to smooth rough edges.

2. Paint frame with acrylic paint in desired color. Frame may need more than one coat. Dry thoroughly.

3. Paint accent details on each frame using elements found in your cards. We used several techniques on our frames. On the pink frame, we used a stencil to add a check design in a lighter shade. We marked vertical lines every ¼" on the blue frame. We then painted very thin lines on marks in a lighter shade of blue. The yellow frame is accented with diamond quilting stitches. Draw diagonal grid lines on frame. Paint dash lines in a darker shade of paint, leaving a space between each dash to give a quilted look. Allow frames to dry thoroughly.

4. Apply matte spray varnish following manufacturer's directions.

# CRIB CANOPY

*Your precious prince or princess will have sweet dreams under this colorful canopy. Our instructions, diagrams, and photos show you how to make this easy project. Softly sculpted moon and stars and a fabric bow provide the finishing touches!*

## Fabric Requirements

Inside Canopy - 2 yards each of three fabrics
Outside Canopy - 3½ yards
Ribbon - various sizes and lengths
Tissue paper - 16-18 sheets
Swag hook
Cup hooks or hangers - 8

## Making the Canopy

**1.** Center a swag hook in ceiling over crib or bed, approximately 15" from wall.

**2.** Cut each piece of fabric in half lengthwise. Sew short ends of matching fabrics together using a French seam or a ⅝" seam. Press to one side.

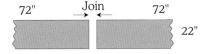

**3.** To finish edges of fabric pieces, turn fabric under ¼" and ¼" again, then stitch around all edges. Press.

**4.** Place center seam on a solid surface and accordion pleat at center seam line from side to side making 1½" pleats. To hold pleats in place, fasten a large clip or clothes pin on each section until all are pleated. Do not press.

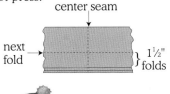

**5.** Stack pleated fabrics together in the desired order placing center fabric on bottom and outside fabric on top. At the center seams, tie fabrics together with 12 inches of ½" ribbon. If desired, attach moon and stars ornament with the same ribbon. Tie ribbon in a secure loop and hang on swag hook. This canopy is planned to hang from a standard eight-foot ceiling. If ceilings are higher, you may want to tie a ribbon to the hook, then to the canopy peak at the desired height.

**6.** Beginning with the fabric section in the center, tie each end of fabric loosely with a cord or ⅜" ribbon about 10" from the hem end. Tape or pin cord to the wall approximately 66"-69" from the floor. This will allow the fabric to balloon. Fold the fabric end or "tail" to the inside of the balloon.

**7.** Continue with the other fabrics securing ties on wall about 6"-8" apart. For the outside panels use an 18" piece of

½"-wide decorative ribbon to tie the fabric panels about 9 feet from each end adjusting as necessary. Temporarily secure in place.

**8.** Slightly crumple tissue paper and place behind fabric to add dimension. We used 2-3 pieces individually for each section of the canopy.

**9.** Adjust fabric as needed. When you are pleased with the arrangement, replace the pins or tape with a cup hook, picture hook, or child-safe hanger.

**10.** Turn under outside fabric panel ends for a soft, relaxed look or hem as desired.

**11.** Tie decorative bow with 1½"-wide ribbon at the top of canopy folds. Our canopy is approximately 41" long from top to lower edges of the balloon. The center of the balloon is 57" from the floor.

## Moon & Stars Ornament

Moon - ¼ yard
Embroidery floss
Hat and Cheek-Star - Scraps
Stars (Felted wool or felt) - Scraps
Ribbon ¼"- ⅜"-wide - Scrap
Heavyweight fusible web - Scrap

Reduce moon pattern from page 8 to 80% and make moon according to directions on page 7.

For the stars, fuse wrong sides of wool together.

Using star pattern on page 8, trace and cut out stars. Attach to moon using double strand of thread. Attach a small ribbon loop to moon and secure to canopy.

**Diagram (step 2):**
72" | Join → ← | 72" | 22"

**Diagram (step 4):**
center seam
next fold → | } 1½" folds

11

# How Tall Am I?

## GROWTH CHART

How Tall Am I? Growth Chart

• Finished Size: 30" x 54½"
Photo on page 14

*A delightful giraffe measures baby's growth through the years making this a wallhanging that will become an heirloom! Embroidered stitches along tree trunk mark off the inches and you can add dimensional leaves to record other vital statistics. The unique border is partially pieced for high impact!*

## Assembling the Panel

This panel is divided into four sections and then the sections are sewn together in rows. The tail, mane, leaves, and butterflies are three-dimensional. Horns, mane, vine, and butterflies are appliquéd. We added a lightweight batting inside the leaves, which we sewed to the quilt through their centers. For measuring growth we stitched ¼-inch and 1-inch marks with a blanket stitch on the side of the tree. Mark your child's name and age on a leaf and

stitch it to the appropriate height on the vine. Just for fun, transfer a photo of your child to fabric and make it the center of a daisy-like blossom to attach to the vine.

In each section you will be making many Quick Corner Triangle units. Refer to page 22 for directions.

## SECTION 1

**1.** Make a quick corner triangle by sewing 7½" Fabric A square to 8½" x 7½" Fabric B piece as shown. Press.

A = 7½ x 7½
B = 8½ x 7½

**2.** Sew unit from step 1 between 8½" Fabric B square and 5½" x 8½" Fabric A piece. Press. Section 1 is complete.

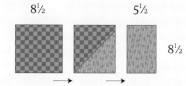

8½          5½

8½

## SECTION 2

**1.** Sew one 1½" Fabric A square to one 8½" x 1½" Fabric B piece to make a quick corner triangle unit as shown. Press.

A = 1½ x 1½
B = 8½ x 1½

**2.** Make a quick corner triangle unit by sewing one 2½" Fabric B square to one 7½" x 6½" Fabric A piece. Press.

B = 2½ x 2½
A = 7½ x 6½

## Fabric Requirements and Cutting Instructions

Before you begin, read Cutting the Strips and Pieces on page 22.

| | First Cut | | Second Cut | |
|---|---|---|---|---|
| | Number of Strips or Pieces | Dimensions | Number of Pieces | Dimensions |
| **Fabric A** Background *7/8 yard* | 1 | 8½" x 42" | 1 | 8½" x 10½" |
| | | | 1 | 6½" x 10½" |
| | | | 5 | 1½" squares |
| | 1 | 7½" x 42" | 1 | 7½" square |
| | | | 3 | 7½" x 6½" |
| | | | 1 | 7½" x 5½" |
| *It is a good idea to label pieces with masking tape noting size.* | 1 | 5½" x 42" | 1 | 5½" x 8½" |
| | | | 1 | 5½" square |
| | | | 2 | 5½" x 3½" |
| | 1 | 4½" x 42" | 1 | 4½" x 9½" |
| | | | 2 | 4½" x 2½" |
| | | | 2 | 4" x 2½" |
| | | | 1 | 3½" x 2½" |
| | | | 1 | 2½" square |
| **Fabric B** Treetop *1/3 yard* | 1 | 8½" x 42" | 1 | 8½" square |
| | | | 1 | 8½" x 7½" |
| | | | 1 | 8½" x 1½" |
| | | | 2 | 2½" squares |
| **Fabric C** Tree Trunk *1/6 yard* | 1 | 4½" x 10½" | | |
| | 1 | 3½" x 10½" | | |
| | 1 | 2½" x 8½" | | |
| | 1 | 2½" x 5½" | | |
| | 1 | 2½" square | | |
| | 1 | 1½" x 4½" | | |
| | 2 | 1½" squares | | |
| **Fabric D** Giraffe *3/8 yard* | 1 | 8½" x 42" | 1 | 8½" square |
| | | | 2 | 8½" x 2½" |
| | | | 1 | 6½" x 2½" |
| | 1 | 3½" x 42" | 1 | 3½" x 10½" |
| | | | 1 | 3½" x 6½" |
| | | | 1 | 3½" x 4½" |
| | | | 1 | 3½" square |
| | | | 3 | 2½" squares |
| | | | 3 | 1½" squares |
| Nose | 1 | 1½" x 4½" | | |
| Hoofs | 2 | 2½" squares | | |
| Horns *scraps* | 2 | 7/8" x 2½" | | |
| **Mane** *1/8 yard* | 1 | 1¼" x 42" | 2 | 1¼" x 13" |
| | | | 2 | 1¼" x 3" |
| **Vine** *1/4 yard* | 5 | 1¼" x 8" bias strips | | |

**3.** Sew one 2½" Fabric B square to one 2½" x 5½" Fabric C piece. Press.

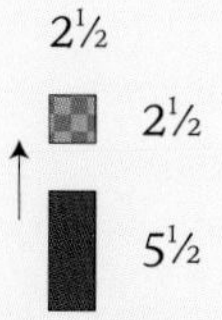

2½

2½

5½

**4.** Sew together units from steps 1, 2, and 3, as shown. Press.

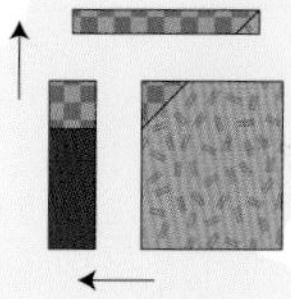

**5.** Sew one 2½" Fabric D square to one 4" x 2½" Fabric A piece to make a quick corner triangle unit. Press.

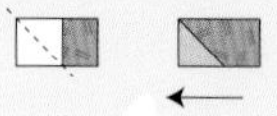

D = 2½ x 2½
A = 4 x 2½

**6.** Join unit from step 5 to one 4" x 2½" Fabric A piece. Press.

4

 2½

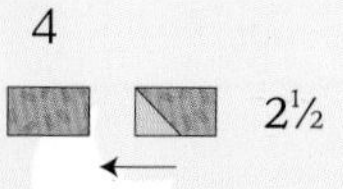

**7.** Sew one 1½" Fabric A square to one 3½" x 6½" Fabric D piece. Press.

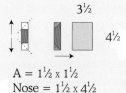

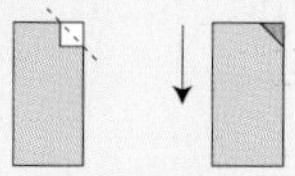

A = 1½ x 1½
D = 3½ x 6½

**8.** Sew two 1½" Fabric A squares to the 1½" x 4½" nose fabric. Press. Join this unit to one 3½" x 4½" Fabric D piece as shown. Press.

3½

4½

A = 1½ x 1½
Nose = 1½ x 4½

**9.** Sew one 1½" Fabric D square to one 4½" x 2½" Fabric A piece. Press.

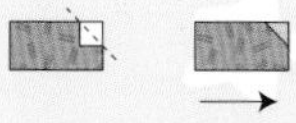

D = 1½ x 1½
A = 2½ x 4½

**10.** Join units from steps 7, 8, and 9 together as shown. Press

**11.** Join units from step 4, 6, and 10 together as shown. Press.

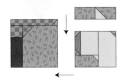

**12.** Refer to layout on page 12 and appliqué the horns to the top of the giraffe's head using two $7/8$" x $2\frac{1}{2}$" horn pieces.

**13.** Make a quick corner triangle by sewing one $2\frac{1}{2}$" Fabric D square to one $5\frac{1}{2}$" Fabric A square. Press. Sew one $5\frac{1}{2}$" x $3\frac{1}{2}$" Fabric A piece to top of unit. Press.

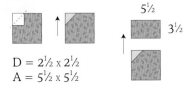

D = $2\frac{1}{2}$ x $2\frac{1}{2}$
A = $5\frac{1}{2}$ x $5\frac{1}{2}$

**14.** Join units from steps 11 and 13 together to complete section 2. Press.

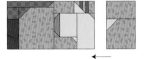

## SECTION 3

**1.** Sew one $3\frac{1}{2}$" Fabric D square to one $5\frac{1}{2}$" x $3\frac{1}{2}$" Fabric A piece to make a quick corner triangle unit. Press.

D = $3\frac{1}{2}$ x $3\frac{1}{2}$
A = $5\frac{1}{2}$ x $3\frac{1}{2}$

**2.** Sew together one $7\frac{1}{2}$" x $5\frac{1}{2}$" Fabric A piece and unit from step 1 as shown. Press and sew that unit to one $3\frac{1}{2}$" x $10\frac{1}{2}$" Fabric D piece. Press.

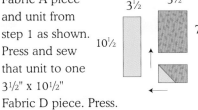

**3.** Sew one $2\frac{1}{2}$" Fabric A square to one $8\frac{1}{2}$" Fabric D square to make a quick corner triangle unit. Press. Join to unit from step 2 as shown. Press.

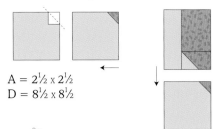

A = $2\frac{1}{2}$ x $2\frac{1}{2}$
D = $8\frac{1}{2}$ x $8\frac{1}{2}$

**4.** Make a quick corner triangle unit by sewing one $1\frac{1}{2}$" Fabric A square to one $3\frac{1}{2}$" x $10\frac{1}{2}$" Fabric C piece. Press.

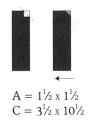

A = $1\frac{1}{2}$ x $1\frac{1}{2}$
C = $3\frac{1}{2}$ x $10\frac{1}{2}$

**5.** Make another quick corner triangle unit by sewing one $2\frac{1}{2}$" Fabric D square to one $4\frac{1}{2}$" x $9\frac{1}{2}$" Fabric A piece. Press.

D = $2\frac{1}{2}$ x $2\frac{1}{2}$
A = $4\frac{1}{2}$ x $9\frac{1}{2}$

**6.** Make a quick corner triangle unit by sewing one $1\frac{1}{2}$" Fabric C square to one $7\frac{1}{2}$" x $6\frac{1}{2}$" Fabric A piece. Press. Sew one $6\frac{1}{2}$" x $2\frac{1}{2}$" Fabric D piece to unit. Press.

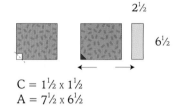

$2\frac{1}{2}$

$6\frac{1}{2}$

C = $1\frac{1}{2}$ x $1\frac{1}{2}$
A = $7\frac{1}{2}$ x $6\frac{1}{2}$

**7.** Sew together units from steps 4, 5, and 6 as shown. Press.

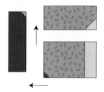

**8.** Sew together one $2\frac{1}{2}$" x $8\frac{1}{2}$" Fabric C piece and one $8\frac{1}{2}$" x $10\frac{1}{2}$" Fabric A piece. Press. Join to unit from step 7. Press. Sew together to unit from step 3 to complete section 3. Press.

$2\frac{1}{2}$   $10\frac{1}{2}$

$8\frac{1}{2}$

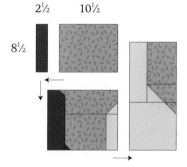

**9.** Add the tail (page 16) now or appliqué it after quilt panel is complete. To make the tail, fold fabric right sides together and stitch a lengthwise seam. Back stitch to secure ends. Turn right side out and stuff lightly, if desired, for dimension. Pin to place where giraffe's body will be sewn to the accent border. Baste and make sure tail is in correct position.

## SECTION 4

**1.** Sew two $1\frac{1}{2}$" Fabric D squares to two corners of one $6\frac{1}{2}$" x $10\frac{1}{2}$" Fabric A piece. Press.

D = $1\frac{1}{2}$ x $1\frac{1}{2}$
A = $6\frac{1}{2}$ x $10\frac{1}{2}$

**2.** Sew two $2\frac{1}{2}$" hoof fabric squares to two $8\frac{1}{2}$" x $2\frac{1}{2}$" Fabric D pieces. Press. Sew these two units to sides of unit from step 1 as shown.

$2\frac{1}{2}$

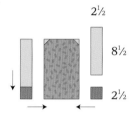

$8\frac{1}{2}$

$2\frac{1}{2}$

**3.** Make a quick corner triangle unit by sewing one $2\frac{1}{2}$" Fabric C square to one $4\frac{1}{2}$" x $2\frac{1}{2}$" Fabric A piece. Press.

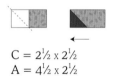

C = $2\frac{1}{2}$ x $2\frac{1}{2}$
A = $4\frac{1}{2}$ x $2\frac{1}{2}$

**4.** Sew unit from step 3 to one $1\frac{1}{2}$" x $4\frac{1}{2}$" Fabric C piece. Press.

$4\frac{1}{2}$

$1\frac{1}{2}$

**5.** Make another quick corner triangle unit by sewing one $1\frac{1}{2}$" Fabric C square to one $3\frac{1}{2}$" x $2\frac{1}{2}$" Fabric A piece. Press.

C = $1\frac{1}{2}$ x $1\frac{1}{2}$
A = $3\frac{1}{2}$ x $2\frac{1}{2}$

**6.** Join units from steps 4 and 5 together as shown. Press. Add one $7\frac{1}{2}$" x $6\frac{1}{2}$" Fabric A piece. Press.

$6\frac{1}{2}$

$7\frac{1}{2}$

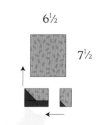

**7.** Sew unit from step 6 between one $4\frac{1}{2}$" x $10\frac{1}{2}$" Fabric C piece and unit from step 2. Press. Section 4 is now complete.

$4\frac{1}{2}$

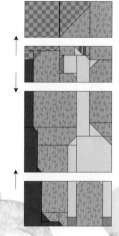

$10\frac{1}{2}$

**8.** Sew together sections 1, 2, 3, and 4 as shown. Press.

**9.** Refer to quilt layout on page 12 and photo for vine placement. Use five $1\frac{1}{4}$" x 8" bias strips of fabric to make the vine. Fold each fabric strip lengthwise, wrong sides together, and press. Determine placement for each vine strip and stitch to tree trunk $\frac{1}{4}$" from strip's raw edges. Press vine strip over seam and appliqué to tree trunk.

**10.** Stack pairs of matching mane pieces with wrong side on top of right side. On each pair, sew a gathering thread $\frac{1}{4}$" away from one long edge. Make $\frac{1}{2}$"-deep cuts about $\frac{1}{4}$" apart along unstitched long edge. Gather short mane strip to fit from horns to ear. Gather long mane strip to fit along neck between ear and back. Press under the seam allowance of both mane strips along the gathered line. Appliqué mane pieces to head and neck of giraffe.

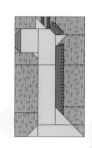

## Adding the Borders

| | First Cut | |
|---|---|---|
| | Number of Strips or Pieces | Dimensions |
| **Borders** | | |
| Grass 1/8 yard | 1 | 1½" x 20½" |
| Accent Border 1/6 yard | 3 | 1½" x 42" |
| Patchwork Border assorted scraps | 72 | 2½" assorted squares |
| Outside Border 1/3 yard | 2 | 4½" x 42" |
| Binding 1/2 yard | 5 | 2¾" x 42" |

Leaves - Assorted green scraps
Butterflies - Assorted scraps
Backing - 1⅔ yards
Batting - 36" x 60"
Embroidery floss
Optional: Button for giraffe eye and tassel for tail

**1.** Sew one 1½" x 20½" strip of grass fabric to the bottom of quilt. Sew 1" x 42" accent border strips end to end to make one continuous 1" strip. Referring to Adding the Borders on page 24, add to the top and sides of quilt.

**2.** Refer to quilt layout on page 12. Sew together seventy-two 2½" squares in pairs then in four sections to make patchwork borders. Sew 4½" outside border fabric strips to the top and bottom patchwork borders to equal 21½". Sew top and bottom outside borders to quilt. Press.

**3.** Measure the quilt from top to bottom through the center including the borders just added. Sew remaining outside border strips to remaining patchwork borders and trim to equal that measurement. Press. Sew outside border strips to sides of quilt. Press.

## Layering and Finishing

**1.** Refer to Layering the Quilt directions on page 24. Baste and quilt panel.

**2.** Referring to Binding the Quilt directions on page 24, sew top and bottom binding to quilt. Cut one binding strip in half and sew one half to each remaining binding strip. Sew to sides of quilt. Press.

**3.** Using a blanket stitch, stitch ¼" and 1" marks on left side of tree trunk.

**4.** Add leaves, butterflies, button for eye, and tassel for tail, if desired.

**5.** To hang, place your first stitched inch mark 24" from the floor. The top of your quilt will be approximately 6' high.

### LEAVES

Trace leaf patterns on page 19 onto template plastic or freezer paper. Place leaf fabric right sides together. Trace around leaf patterns on fabric, making sure leaves are ½" apart. Lay on top of lightweight batting. Stitch on drawn lines through all three layers. Cut leaves apart leaving a scant ¼" seam. Cut a slit through one layer of fabric and turn leaves right side out. Press. Place leaves on tree-top and stitch in place through center of leaves to resemble a center vein.

### BUTTERFLIES

**1.** Trace butterfly patterns from this page. Place wing pattern on fold of fabric. Cut out butterfly. Stitch butterfly piece, right sides together, leaving an opening to turn. Turn right side out and press. Slipstitch opening.

**2.** Sew a line of gathers through center of wings, and gather to measure 1½".

**3.** Cut out butterfly body piece and stitch. Clip corners, turn, press, and slip stitch. Hand or machine stitch to center of wings. Repeat steps 1–3 to make two. Slipstitch butterflies to quilt. If desired, embroider butterfly antennae.

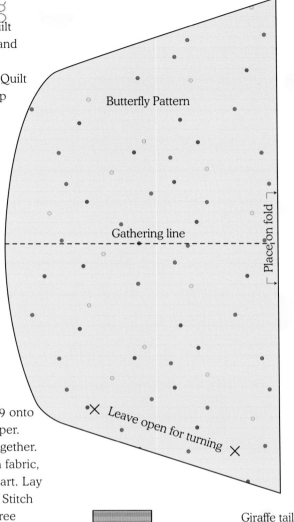

Butterfly Pattern

Gathering line

Place on fold

✕ Leave open for turning ✕

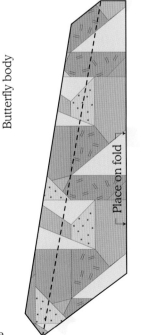

Giraffe tail

Leave open for turning

Place on fold

Butterfly body

Place on fold

# Hide & Seek
## WALL QUILT

Hide & Seek Wall Quilt
*Finished Size: 38½" x 30½"*

*Baby will have hours of fun searching this wallhanging for the hidden animals!
A variety of animals are carefully camouflaged in the landscape of this watercolor
technique quilt. The quilt is simple to sew, but it may take some time to select the fabric!*

## Fabric Requirements and Cutting Instructions

Before you begin, read Cutting the Strips and Pieces on page 22.
Squares - One Hundred Ninety Two
   2½" squares
Accent Border (¼ yard) - Four
   1¼" x 42" strips
Border (⅓ yard) - Four 2½" x 42" strips
Binding (⅜ yard) - Four 2¾" x 42" strips
Animals - Assorted scraps
Backing - 1 yard
Batting - 42½" x 34½"
2½"–Grid Interfacing - 1¼ yards
Fusible Web - ½ yard

## Selecting Fabrics

Watercolor quilts are pictorial quilts made from squares of fabrics. You will need a variety of fabrics that contain different designs, motif scales, colors, and values. Fabric with leaves, flowers, vines, and busy prints work well and be sure to use a variety of "blender" fabrics to help you transition between colors. You will be cutting more fabric than required to get that special look to your quilt, adding and eliminating fabric as needed. Let your fabric stash determine the final look of your quilt.

## Assembly

**1.** Place 2½" grid interfacing on table or design wall with adhesive side up. You will place wrong side of assorted 2½" squares of watercolor fabrics on adhesive side of interfacing.

**2.** Arrange 2½" fabric squares in a pleasing manner following quilt photo as a guide.

**3.** When satisfied with the arrangement of squares, press wrong side of squares to grid interfacing following manufacturer's directions.

**4.** Fold right sides together at marked lines. Stitch according to manufacturer's sewing instructions.

## Appliqué

Refer to Quick-Fuse Appliqué directions on page 23. Trace appliqué designs from pages 18-19. Referring to color photo for placement, quick-fuse appliqués to quilt.

## Borders

**1.** Measure quilt through center from side to side. Cut two 1¼" accent border strips to that measurement. Sew to top and bottom. Press seams toward border strips.

**2.** Measure quilt through center from top to bottom, including borders just added. Cut two 1¼" accent border strips to that measurement. Sew to sides of quilt. Press seams toward border strips.

**3.** Repeat steps 1 and 2 to add 2½" outside border strips to quilt.

## Layering and Finishing

**1.** Referring to Layering the Quilt directions on page 24, arrange and baste backing, batting, and top together.

**2.** Machine or hand quilt as desired.

**3.** Sew 2¾" x 42" binding strips to quilt referring to Binding the Quilt directions on page 24.

Tracing Line _____

Tracing Line - - - - - - - - - - - -
*(will be hidden behind other fabrics)*

Pillow Star

*Tracing Line* _____

*Tracing Line* _ _ _ _ _ _ _ _ _ _ _ _
*(will be hidden behind other fabrics)*

Leaves for
How Tall am I?
Growth Chart

Small leaf pattern
(light green)

Large leaf pattern (dark green)

# CRIB QUILT

**Zany Zoo Crib Quilt**

*Finished Size: 43" x 63"*
*Photo on page 21*

*Lions, monkeys, giraffes, oh my! A zany zoo of animals highlights the blocks
on this easily constructed crib quilt. Animals are appliquéd to the
pieced quilt that features a printed border.*

## Making the Blocks

You will make eight of Block 1 (two each of four different colors), and seven
of Block 2 with animal appliqués. The appliqués are quick-fused and satin
stitched, but may be hand appliquéd or stitched in another manner. Facial
details are embroidered. Refer to Assembly Line directions on page 22 to
piece the blocks. Press in the direction of the arrows.

### Block 1 (Make eight)

**1.** Sew one 2½" x 4½" Fabric A
piece between two 4½" Fabric B
squares. Press. Make sixteen, four of
each color.

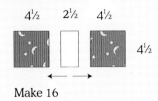

Make 16
(4 each color)

**2.** Sew one 2½" Fabric C square
between two 2½" x 4½" Fabric A
pieces. Press. Make eight.

Make 8

**3.** Sew one unit from step 2
between two units from step 1. Press.
Make eight.

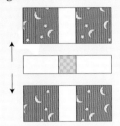

Make 8

### Block 2 (Make seven)

Following Quick Corner Triangle
directions on page 22, sew four 4½"
Fabric D squares to each 10½"
Fabric A square. Press. Make seven.

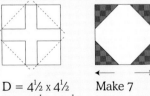

D = 4½ x 4½        Make 7
A = 10½ x 10½

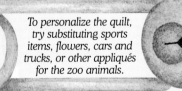

*To personalize the quilt,
try substituting sports
items, flowers, cars and
trucks, or other appliqués
for the zoo animals.*

# Fabric Requirements and Cutting Instructions

Before you begin, read Cutting the Strips and Pieces on page 22.

| | First Cut | | Second Cut | |
| --- | --- | --- | --- | --- |
| | Number of Strips or Pieces | Dimensions | Number of Pieces | Dimensions |
| Fabric A Block 2 background and Block 1 strips 1 1/4 yards | 3 | 10 1/2" x 42" | 7 | 10 1/2" squares |
| | 4 | 2 1/2" x 42" | 32 | 2 1/2" x 4 1/2" |
| Fabric B Block 1 corners 1/6 yard each of four different colors | 1* | 4 1/2" x 42" | 8* | 4 1/2" squares |
| | *Repeat for each color | | *Repeat for each color | |
| Fabric C Block 1 centers 1/8 yard | 1 | 2 1/2" x 42" | 8 | 2 1/2" squares |
| Fabric D Block 2 corners 5/8 yard | 4 | 4 1/2" x 42" | 28 | 4 1/2" squares |

| | First Cut | |
| --- | --- | --- |
| | Number of Strips or Pieces | Dimensions |
| Borders | | |
| Accent Border 1/4 yard | 5 | 1" x 42" |
| Middle Border 3/8 yard | 5 | 2" x 42" |
| Outside Border 3/4 yard | 5 | 4 1/2" x 42" |
| Binding 5/8 yard | 6 | 2 3/4" x 42" |

Backing - 3 yards
Batting - 50" x 70"
Lightweight Fusible Web - 1/2 yard

# Assembly

Refer to quilt layout on page 20 and color photo. Alternating Blocks 1 and 2, arrange blocks in five rows with three blocks in each row. Press seams toward Block 2. Join rows and press.

Odd rows
(colors will vary)

Even rows
(colors will vary)

# General Directions

*(Zany Zoo Crib Quilt continued)*

## Adding the Borders

1. Measure quilt from side to side through the center of quilt. Cut two 1" x 42" accent border strips to that measurement. Sew to top and bottom of quilt. Press seams toward border strips.

2. Cut one 1" x 42" accent border strip in half. Sew to one end of each remaining accent border strip.

3. Measure quilt through center from top to bottom including borders just added. Cut accent border strips to that measurement and sew to sides. Press.

4. Repeat steps 1, 2, and 3 to add 2" x 42" middle border strips to top and bottom, then sides of quilt. Press.

5. Repeat steps 1, 2, and 3 to add 4½" x 42" outside border strips to top, bottom, and sides of quilt. Press.

## Appliqués

Referring to quilt layout on page 20, trace animal appliqué designs from pages 18-19. Quick-fuse or hand appliqué animals to quilt top, following directions on page 23. Add facial features with embroidery or fine-tip permanent pen.

## Layering and Finishing

1. Cut backing fabric in half crosswise and sew together to make one 50" x 70" (approximate) backing piece. Arrange and baste backing, batting, and quilt top together referring to Layering the Quilt directions on page 24.

2. Machine or hand quilt as desired.

3. Sew 2¾" x 42" binding strips together end to end. Refer to Binding the Quilt directions on page 24 to finish.

## Cutting the Strips and Pieces

Before you make each of the projects in this book, pre-wash and press the fabrics. Using rotary cutter, see-through ruler, and cutting mat, cut the strips and pieces for the project. If indicated on the Cutting Chart, some will need to be cut again into smaller strips and pieces. The approximate width of the fabric is 42". Measurements for all pieces include ¼"-wide seam allowance unless otherwise indicated. Press in the direction of the arrows.

## Assembly Line Method

Whenever possible, use the assembly line method. Position pieces right sides together and line up next to sewing machine. Stitch first unit together, then continue sewing others without breaking threads. When all units are sewn, clip threads to separate. Press in direction of arrows.

## Embroidery Stitch Guide

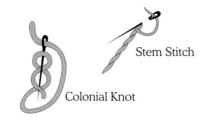

Stem Stitch

Colonial Knot

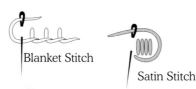

Blanket Stitch

Satin Stitch

French Knot

## Quick Corner Triangles

Quick corner triangles are formed by simply sewing fabric squares to other squares and rectangles. The directions and diagrams with each project show you what size pieces to use and where to place squares on corresponding piece. Follow steps 1–3 below to make corner triangle units.

1. With pencil and ruler, draw diagonal line on wrong side of fabric square that will form the triangle. See Diagram A. This will be your sewing line.

A.

sewing line

2. With right sides together, place square on corresponding piece. Matching raw edges, pin in place and sew ON drawn line. Trim off excess fabric leaving ¼" seam allowance as shown in Diagram B.

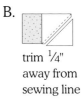

B.

trim ¼"
away from
sewing line

3. Press seam in direction of arrow as shown in step-by-step project diagram. Measure completed corner triangle unit to ensure greatest accuracy.

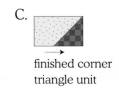

C.

finished corner
triangle unit

## Quick-Fuse Appliqué

Quick-fuse appliqué is a method of adhering appliqué pieces to a background with fusible web. For quick and easy results, simply quick-fuse appliqué pieces in place. Use sewable, lightweight fusible web for the projects in this book unless indicated otherwise. Finishing raw edges with stitching is desirable. Laundering is not recommended unless edges are finished.

1. With paper side up, lay fusible web over appliqué design. Leaving ½" space between pieces, trace all elements of design. Cut around traced pieces, approximately ¼" outside traced line.

A.
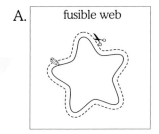
fusible web

2. With paper side up, position and iron fusible web to wrong side of selected fabrics. Follow manufacturer's directions for iron temperature and fusing time. Cut out each piece on traced line.

B.
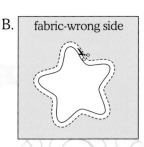
fabric-wrong side

3. Remove paper backing from pieces. A thin film will remain on wrong side. Position and fuse all pieces of one appliqué design at a time onto background, referring to color photos for placement.

## Hand Appliqué

Hand appliqué is easy when you start out with the right supplies. Cotton or machine embroidery thread is easy to work with. Pick a color that matches the appliqué fabric as closely as possible. Use appliqué or silk pins for holding shapes in place, and a long, thin needle, like a sharp, for stitching.

1. Make a plastic template for every shape in the appliqué design. Use a dotted line to show where pieces overlap.

2. Place template on right side of appliqué fabric. Trace around template.

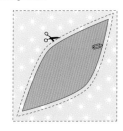

3. Cut out shapes ¼" beyond traced line.

4. Position shapes on background fabric. Pin shapes in place.

5. Stitch shapes that go underneath first. Where shapes overlap, do not turn under and stitch edges of bottom pieces. Turn and stitch the edges of the piece on top.

6. Use the traced line as your turn-under guide. Entering from the wrong side of the appliqué shape, bring the needle up on the traced line. Using the tip of the needle, turn under the fabric along the traced line.  Using blind stitch, stitch along the folded edge to join the appliqué shape to the background fabric. Turn under and stitch about ¼" at a time.

## Machine Appliqué

This technique should be used when you are planning to launder quick-fuse projects. Several different stitches can be used: small narrow zigzag stitch, satin stitch, blanket stitch, or another decorative machine stitch. Use an appliqué foot if your machine has one. Use a tear-away stabilizer or water-soluble stabilizer to obtain even stitches and help prevent puckering. Always practice first to adjust your machine settings.

1. Fuse all pieces following Quick-Fuse Appliqué directions.

2. Cut a piece of stabilizer large enough to extend beyond the area you are stitching. Pin to the wrong side of fabric.

3. Select thread to match appliqué.

4. Following the order that appliqués were positioned, stitch along the edges of each section. Anchor beginning and ending stitches by tying off or stitching in place two or three times.

5. Complete all stitching, then remove stabilizers.

## Product Resource List

Debbie Mumm® products featured in this book were provided by the following companies:

Wallpaper – Imperial Home Décor Group, (800) 539-5399 www.imp-wall.com

Baby Books & Frames – Brownlow, (800) 433-7610 www.brownlowgift.com

Greeting Cards – AMCAL, (800) 824-5879 www.amcalart.com

Infant Bedding and Accessories – Kids Line, Inc., (310) 660-0110 www.kidsline.com

For more information on Debbie Mumm® products, please visit our website at www.debbiemumm.com, call toll free (888) 819-2923, or (509) 466-3572.

## Adding the Borders

1. Measure quilt through the center from side to side. Cut two border strips to this measurement. Sew to top and bottom of quilt. Press toward border.

2. Measure quilt through the center from top to bottom, including the border added in step 1. Cut side border strips to this measurement. Sew to sides and press. Repeat to add additional borders.

## Mitered Borders

1. Cut the border strips as indicated for each quilt.

2. Measure each side of the quilt and mark center with a pin. Fold each border unit crosswise to find its midpoint and mark with a pin. Using the side measurements, measure out from the midpoint of border and place a pin to show where the edges of the quilt will be.

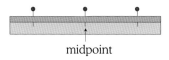

midpoint

3. Align a border unit to quilt. Pin at midpoints and pin-marked ends first, then along entire side, easing to fit if necessary.

4. Sew border to quilt, stopping and starting ¼" from pinmarked end points. Repeat to sew all four border units to quilt.

quilt front

5. Fold corner of quilt diagonally, right sides together, matching seams and borders. Place a long ruler along fold line extending across border. Draw a diagonal line across border from fold to edge of border. This is the stitching line. Starting at ¼" mark, stitch on drawn line. Check for squareness, then trim excess. Press seam open.

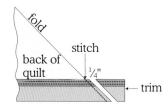

fold

stitch

back of quilt

¼"

← trim

## Layering the Quilt

1. Cut backing and batting 4" to 8" larger than quilt top.

2. Lay pressed backing on bottom (right side down), batting in middle, and pressed quilt top (right side up) on top. Make sure everything is centered and that backing and batting are flat. Backing and batting will extend beyond quilt top.

3. Begin basting in center and work toward outside edges. Baste vertically and horizontally, forming a 3"–4" grid. Baste or pin completely around edge of quilt top. Quilt as desired. Remove basting.

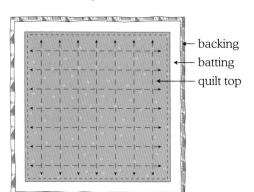

backing

batting

quilt top

## Binding the Quilt

1. Trim batting and backing to ¼" from raw edge of quilt top.

2. Fold and press binding strips in half lengthwise with wrong sides together.

3. Lay binding strips on top and bottom edges of quilt top with raw edges of binding and quilt top aligned. Sew through all layers, ¼" from quilt edge. Press binding away from quilt top. Trim excess length of binding.

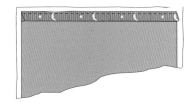

4. Sew remaining two binding strips to quilt sides. Press and trim excess length.

5. Folding top and bottom first, fold binding around to back then repeat with sides. Press and pin in position. Hand stitch binding in place.

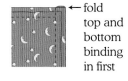

← fold top and bottom binding in first